COMMON GROUNDS

The Art of Relational Selling
SERVE FIRST. START SMALL.

ANCIL LEA
WITH AMY RICHARD AND FRIENDS

Foreword by Quinn Loftis

Common Grounds 2: The Art of Relational Selling
by Ancil Lea and Friends

Amazon ISBN: 9798844623950

Cover Design: Raye Allison

Copyright ©2022 James Henry Books, LLC. All rights reserved.

Connect with me:
www.ancillea.com
www.linkedin.com/in/ancillea/

COMMON GROUNDS
2

The Art of Relational Selling
SERVE FIRST. START SMALL.

ANCIL LEA
WITH AMY RICHARD AND FRIENDS
Foreword by Quinn Loftis

Contents

Forward..i
About the Author.......................................v
Relational Selling Philosophy..........................3
Why Relational Selling?................................7
Lessons Learned in my Twelve Years....................13
Listening..19
Human Relationships in Sales.........................27
Inquiring > Advocating...............................33
The Pitch..37
Insight & Client-Focus...............................43
Validation...49
Being Known and Trusted..............................53
Building Trust in the Basics.........................55
How Relationships Broke the Internet.................61
Secret Sauce...65
Stories from the Field...............................69
Power in Collaboration...............................73
One more call..79
A Handwritten Letter.................................87
Growing Your Circle of Influence.....................93
Mentoring..97
Toad Suck Daze......................................101
My Story — Helping Children in Need.................105
Wrapping Up...111
You Can Make A Difference...........................113
Aperitif..115

Forward

BY QUINN LOFTIS
USA TODAY BEST-SELLING AUTHOR

There are no werewolves in *Common Grounds 2*. And while this book is about relationships, there is very little romance involved. And I don't think the target audience of Common Grounds 2 is teenage girls, though they'd certainly benefit from reading it. So, how does a woman known for writing fiction—young adult paranormal romance novels—to be specific, come to write a foreword for a nonfiction book about relational selling? As you'll read throughout this book, the key to meaningful relationships is sharing the small things. The 'small thing' Ancil and I had in common is that we are both writers, and we had a mutual friend who thought we should meet. We initially met, as you might imagine if you've read the first Common Grounds, in a coffee shop. And as our friend expected, we hit it off.

Strangely enough, I rarely work in coffee shops, which causes many of my fellow fiction writers to gasp and clutch their pearls. My daily routine usually consists of taking my children to school, then returning home, secluding myself into my office, and attempting to write as many quality words as I can. Some days, there is little relationship involved. I can only imagine this type of work day is about as far from Ancil's typical day as one could get. Despite this, Ancil and I have much in common. We've built a business doing what we love, and we couldn't have done that without the help of others. As a writer, I depend on a host of other people to help me transform my ideas into finished novels. I need an editor, a cover designer, and a marketer, just to name a few. Further, discussions and collaborations with other authors help me hone my craft. As iron sharpens iron, so one author sharpens another. Relationships with my colleagues call me to be humble and thankful as I do whatever I can to help them in their own careers.

It didn't take me long to realize that Ancil is a natural at understanding people. He has a passion for people in both a personal and business capacity. He cares, and it shows. This passion doesn't just show up in the success Ancil has had in business, but in the quality of relationships he's developed along the way. After reading this book, you'll understand how developing these relationships will help you succeed in the arena of sales, but perhaps in an entirely different way than you might expect.

So many transactions in the internet age occur completely in front of a screen, requiring no human interaction. Reservations are made, and everything from bananas to automobiles are purchased without ever even speaking to another person. Don't get me wrong, the benefits of online commerce are many and varied, and I enjoy using the app to have my groceries delivered as much as the next person, but something is missing in our day-to-day hustle and bustle. The art of building relationships has become lost. And while the skill may be lost, the importance of building relationships remains as vital as ever. In fact, I would argue that relationship building has become even more important with fewer and fewer human interactions in our everyday lives.

Common Grounds 2 explores why fostering relationships can do more for us than simply garnering a sale. No matter which area of our lives we are talking about, relationships matter. I am honored to be a small part of Ancil's professional journey, and that he has taken the time to be a part of mine.

So, grab a cup of coffee, settle into a comfortable chair, and dive into the journey of building relationships for your success and the success of those you meet. It is worth stepping out of your comfort zone. This journey will challenge you to help others. Perhaps, one day, through a relationship one of us has built, you and I will find ourselves in each other's paths and experience the blessing of helping one another achieve success.

God bless you and yours,
Quinn Loftis

About the Author

Ancil Lea has been in the software and healthcare business for over thirty-four years. He's seen the rise of healthtech more acutely than many, working daily to help the medical world meet their advancing needs. From helping the State of Arkansas implement the HiTech Act to assisting dozens of medical facilities in choosing the best software to meet their needs, Ancil has navigated this healthtech world and continues to assist others in navigating it as well. Through it all, the backbone of Ancil's work remains the same as that of his life—relationships.

Ancil's learned to see value in people before ever knowing their job title. The person next to you at the coffee shop, no matter their age, occupation, or dress code, may always be someone you can learn and benefit from—and who may be waiting for someone like you to come alongside them! This backbone of relationships has fueled Ancil's work in the sales industry. A natural entrepreneur, Ancil started his own company in 1991, going on to sell it in the early 2000's. And while start-ups are his current passion, he's worked widely in the healthcare technology industry across the mid-South since launching his career.

More than simply making connections, Ancil keeps connections. He remembers the oft-forgotten pieces of a person's life. He asks how he can help, seeking to truly listen to their needs above his agenda. Whether writing on healthcare for various publications or having a chat with someone over a cup of coffee, Ancil's goal is truly to help whoever is on the other side of the table succeed.

It's this relational attitude that sets Ancil apart. Alan Dial, creator of the HealthTech startup StaffDX, commented simply that Ancil is a relationship builder. Having connected with Ancil for help selling his own product, Alan quickly saw a difference in Ancil's approach. "When [Ancil talks] to clients, the climate is very different from what you see in traditional sales ... he doesn't create a pressured environment." The clients in Ancil's circle truly trust his advice, because they trust the long-term relationship.

Relational selling through Ancil allowed StaffDX to move forward in what's arguably the hardest step for any start-up: from zero clients to one. And then some. "Since we started working together [after just a year], StaffDX is in front of and collaborating with more clients than I could have wished for," states Alan.

The success of Alan's product and many other start-ups is not due to gimmicks, perfect pitches, or seamless sales funnels. It's due to relationships.

Serving others has been the hallmark of Ancil's career. He believes that growing contacts must be through intentionally serving others. In this book you'll find out how he does it.

"To get, you must first give."

So, let's begin.

Relational Selling

Relational Selling Philosophy

BY ANCIL LEA

About four years ago I was asked to work on a project with a venture organization associated with a large specialty hospital. The solution they were developing was meant to reduce readmissions for their patients, and I was honored to come alongside them to figure out if their product was viable and marketable. As I engaged in the project, I got to know several of the key players that were part of this project. One of these was an older multi-millionaire—we'll call him Rob—who I worked with often, as he was the driving force behind the project.

At one point, he asked me to meet him at Panera for a cup of coffee to review our progress. During the course of the conversation, he said, "You know, Ancil"—he'd gotten to know me well enough that he had sized me up already—"you really like to help people." Then he went on to say, "But you need to help yourself." I kind of chuckled inside at the time, but I later thought about his point. And I thought, well, part of that's true. However, my philosophy all along has been that if I help people, I actually will help myself. That is, if I help people achieve their goals, their dreams, their objectives, it will, in turn, bless me and my firm. And I've witnessed that proved true time and time again.

We live in a very transactional, electronic world, yet what I was taught and truly believe is that the success of the other person and my success go hand in hand. In their success and in genuinely caring about them, their families, etc., I find success, too. As you look at selling or at thriving in any career for that matter, you must consider this methodology or philosophy. If you don't, your selling may come across very cold and very transactional. And that, my friend, is not the way to gain clients.

People want to do business with people they like. Whether that's a mantra I learned at IBM or a truism that I've simply learned throughout these years, it's held up to the test of time.

Helping the other person goes beyond simply filling an order or pitching a product—no matter how useful the product may be. And being liked by potential clients or prospects takes more than a few quick conversations. It takes paying attention to the small things as you develop a real relationship with them. These so-called "small things" are key to all of us. Small things are remembering that so-and-so's daughter is in soccer and asking how she's doing. Small things are being able to listen when people hit hard times, whether it be the death of a parent or struggles in their lives. A relational selling philosophy means the other person feels free to share these "small things" with you. In these moments, you can pray for them (which is an honor to do). You can send them encouraging correspondence whether emails or texts just to check on them to see how they're doing. You can gain more than just a client.

In many ways it seems to me that we have lost this philosophy of really caring for and loving our neighbor as ourselves. Yet it's so greatly needed. Our world and our work need us to care about each other and support each other. As difficult as this life is sometimes, that's the only way we'll make it through together: with friendships and relationships that we can count on even beyond the business world.

May we all look for opportunities to sit down, have a cup of coffee, and share some common grounds.

Why Relational Selling?

BY ANCIL LEA

When I was growing up, my mom always told me, "Son, you'd make a great salesperson." Despite her words, that was never the consideration I had in those early years. I always wanted to be something else, you know, perhaps a doctor?

Even so, as a senior in high school I started working at a men's fine clothing store in downtown Conway, Arkansas. There I discovered something: I really was good at sales. And I wondered, as I finished up high school and entered my first year of college, what I would end up doing, with sales now sitting in the back of my mind.

I finished my degree at Ouachita Baptist University, but I hadn't decided to study business. Or economics. Or marketing. I ended up focusing on history and political science—nothing at all dealing with sales. Neither had I gotten any sales training while in college. Two weeks before I was to finish my degree, however, I got a call from my sister's ex-boyfriend who was leaving a job selling medical software. He asked if I would like to be considered for the position.

And I thought, absolutely! I didn't have any other prospects lined up and I needed a job. I'd definitely give it a shot. That's how I started my career in medical software sales.

My initial company gave me very little training, but I found I could use a lot of my skills and experience from selling clothing back in high school toward selling medical software. I knew even then that sales was really more geared around building trusted relationships than anything else.

The industry of medical software technology is highly complex. And the world of healthcare is equally as daunting—clinics and hospitals and surgery centers all operate uniquely. Both have changed in complexity throughout the years as the government has become more and more involved in regulating and reimbursing this industry of healthcare.

But what I find is that even in this difficult atmosphere, there's never a better move than being kind and helpful. Always helping the client get what they need simply requires common sense and kindness. Getting to know somebody—getting to know what their goals are, what their objectives are, and what their fears are, too—allows you to help them address those specifics with solutions.

In this book, relational selling is based around really getting to know people. It's the idea that the individual and what's important to them is the most crucial aspect of the sales process. Therefore spending time with the individual is critical, whether it's face to face or on a virtual call or however. And taking one more step, I'd argue that getting to know what's important to your prospective client and/or your clients even after you sell to them is vital. You must maintain a line of communication (aka, relationship!), so that when they have other needs or when you have other solutions to bring before them, you are able to do so.

One of the more recent large engagements I worked on was with a hospital; we were going through an O.R. management selection and implementation process. It was a long, drawn-out process spanning over a couple years. By the very end of it, I knew I had underpriced myself. But I had done so purposefully. Here's why: The CEO came to me after the whole project was over and beautifully done (much to the credit of the team we had) and she said bluntly, "You did not charge us enough for the work you did." I told her I realized that, but that wasn't really my goal. My real goal was to build a client, a premier client. Now, as she said the other day on a call, "You know, I'll always take your phone call. I'll listen to what you have to say because I trust you." In fact, she just engaged me to help her on a new project.

And that's such a key thing, this thing of trust.

As a matter of fact, trust is critical to relational selling. Because if you ever lose the trust, you've lost a client. You've lost a friend. It takes a long time to build this kind of trust-based client, and you can lose it very quickly. You have to be careful and watchful to both create and maintain trust—to create and maintain relationships.

My hope in this relational selling book is that we realize we're all salespeople. Whether you're working in medical software technology or whether you're a high school counselor or, hey, even if you're a graphic artist or whatever—we're all salespeople, presenting our ideas and trying to persuade. And relational selling works in all of these situations. It is an art; the art of getting to know what really drives the other person and helping them reach their goals.

I hope to give you principles you can use to be successful at whatever position you're in, so that you, too, can help people.

"You can have everything in life you want, if you will just help other people get what they want." - Zig Ziglar

Lessons Learned in my Twelve Years

BY GRANT LUKE

I met Ancil back when I worked for a start-up company in the ambulatory surgery center industry, and we hit it off almost immediately. Our love of family, faith, and fellowship helped us generate rapport quickly, not to mention our love of doing business at coffee shops. Our thoughts aligned on several aspects of our professional careers, and we have been friends ever since. When he asked me to write something for this book, I was humbled that he thought I actually had something to say or could contribute in any meaningful way.

The following will be my best attempt at summing up twelve years of my work. Apologies in advance!

I highly doubt that any kid would say "Salesperson!" if you asked them what they wanted to be when they grow up. I know I didn't! I wanted to be a professional baseball player and was blessed to play all the way through college.

For some reason when people, even kids, think of Sales, they usually think of a scene from a movie:

> Bernie Mac being a used car salesman in "Transformers."
> Jordan Belfort selling penny stocks in "Wolf of Wall Street."
> Alec Baldwin saying "Coffee's for closers" in "Glengarry Ross."
> Chris Farley talking about a warranty in "Tommy Boy."

These pop-culture references create a stigma, or stereotype, about salespeople that most everyone adopts. It usually looks or sounds something like this:

"Salespeople will say anything to get the deal."
"They manipulate you to do something you don't want to do."
"Slick salespeople only care about making the next deal, and not about follow up."

After more than eleven years in sales, I can say I've heard a lot of these thrown my way, even from family members and friends who have never been on a call with me or seen my day-to-day activity. If you are in any kind of sales, I'm sure you can relate to this.

This might be the biggest thing I try to convey in writing this—sales, when done right and effectively over time with success, is not about money, power, or even recognition. Sales, above all else, is about helping others while creating a life for yourself to provide for others.

Whether it be Zig Ziglar, Chris Voss, or Gary Sandler, there are so many great resources on sales and sales success out there that there is little to zero chance I can share something new. Those giants of industry are much more eloquent and smarter than me, not to mention they can forget 99% of what they've learned and still school me in the art of sales. The only thing I can offer is my own personal experience of what sales has taught me, because after all, there isn't a "Grant Luke's Sales Book" or "Luke's School of Sales" out there (at least not yet!).

As best as I can, I will lay out what a life in Sales has taught me:

ONE: Anyone can be in sales.

I start this off by comparing myself to my own brother. We have similar interests, but when it comes to personalities, we couldn't be more different. I enjoy being around people and it really energizes me; I'm your typical extrovert. My brother, on the other hand, struggles with being in a crowd for too long, and it takes effort for him to be around a lot of people. But guess what, both of us have had tremendous careers in sales. We may be different in almost every way, but we both care about people and have a strong work ethic. You see that's the beauty of this job, it doesn't matter your personality, your background, or even your formal education. If you can show up everyday and make your best effort while caring about the people you serve in your industry, sales is a great place to be.

TWO: Being in sales means freedom.

Over my twelve years in sales I have been blessed to work remotely due to my position. Now don't get me wrong, that freedom would've disappeared in a heartbeat had I not been making my number. To me, freedom to live life outside of work, spend time with family, develop meaningful relationships with friends, and give to the local community through my church, always meant more to me than making more money. Of course we need money to live, survive, and provide for others, but I have always been a "work to live" kind of person, and sales has allowed me to do that.

THREE: In sales, if you talk more than the other person, you're doing it wrong.

This struck me when I first entered into the workforce, because admittedly, I had a very stereotypical view of what sales looked like. I kept thinking, "people buy from people they like," and that meant saying the right things and being talkative. However, I was fortunate to have some good training from my managers, and I realized the number one thing I thought made a good salesperson actually made them the worst.

Sales is about asking the right questions more than saying the right thing. Asking a question, and then intently listening to the response, has led to more success for me than any turn of phrase or quippy reply. As you ask questions, you soon realize that the person you are talking to may have a real problem that's severely affecting their business. You begin to gain empathy for their plight and in turn you can help solve their problem.

The great thing about this takeaway is it applies to all your relationships! Whether it be friendship, marriage, or management, if you lack curiosity and fail to ask questions and listen, those relationships will suffer.

FOUR: The best salespeople offer so much more than just their line of products.

I was on a call one day and walked into the CFO's office, ready to have a business discussion. As I walked in, I heard him angrily get off the phone and could visibly see the veins in his neck popping out. Instead of going straight into business talk, I asked, "Hey, is everything ok?" He replied tersely, "Yes—what did you want to talk about?" Instead of diving straight into a line of questioning, I merely asked "Would you rather have this meeting at that coffee shop downstairs?"

The look on his face and the ensuing conversation that took place was worth more to me than making the sale that day. Turns out he was very stressed at work and at home and hadn't had a break all day, and a coffee was just what the doctor ordered. We talked more about golf, NFL teams, and current events than anything to do with the job, and we barely even covered the product I was there for. I didn't make the sale that day, but two weeks later he called and ended up buying everything in our portfolio. I say that to help remind everyone that we deal with people, their emotions, their personalities, their problems, their environment, and their history.

If we are more concerned about people, all of a sudden we become much more valuable than a person pitching a product. We become a trusted partner, a valued asset, a subject matter expert, their "go-to" person. I truly believe I've made more sales because I didn't talk about the product but focused on the person, even to the extent of volunteering free help, connecting them with another expert, or telling them, "You know what, this product really isn't the best fit." If I'm going to have only one interaction with a person on any given day, I want them to leave thinking they are really glad I stopped by.

FIVE: Sales is a failure sport.

I was blessed to play baseball all the way through college, and because of my chosen profession, I thank the Lord I did! You see, in baseball, if you are successful three out of ten times when batting, you're more than likely on your way to the Hall of Fame. Now imagine that same ratio but when passing a class, or answering the phone for customer support, completing an IT project, or having a successful surgery. It just doesn't work out. But in sales, if you are successful one out of ten times in securing a meeting on a cold call, that is something to brag about!

My first year in sales I averaged about 25-35 cold calls per day for three years. You want to talk about a failure sport! But the lessons I learned in baseball helped prepare me for the grind. I couldn't think about that last missed sale, saying something wrong, or just flat out messing up. I had to learn and move on, adapt and overcome. Sales can be very stressful and definitely isn't for everyone, but if you can have the mentality of a baseball player, all of a sudden it puts you in a better mindset to understand that failure is not really failure but a lesson learned for the next at bat.

I'll end with this—I believe way too often companies focus on the details of the sales pitch and product information and forget about the salesperson themselves. If I could change anything about sales training, first and foremost I would focus on the person themselves, and ask them questions. If the person is coming from a sound place mentally, spiritually, and physically, investing in something other than themselves, creating a life and building relationships outside of work, always striving to help others, and never satisfied with the status quo, trust me when I say you won't have to worry about them hitting quota.

Thank you so much for taking the time (or coffee break) to read through this. I hope it gave you a little glimpse into the wonderful world of sales or at least a little empathy for the person on the other line during that next car warranty call.

Listening

BY ANCIL LEA

When I first started my career in the world of selling medical software over thirty-four years ago, there were two things I realized right out of the chute. One: that straight out of college, I hadn't learned anything about the world of healthcare. And two: I didn't really understand the world of technology either. It was all so new! Even so, I somehow managed to set sales records for systems that were sold that year. Now, how in the world did I do that?

Part of what I did—and there's a proverb that speaks to this—was getting really good at listening. I just listened to the customer and what they wanted, then connected them with the solution and, heck, got the people who knew what they were talking about to actually do the demonstration! Then all I had to do was follow-up with the research to actually put the system together and price it out. The proverb I mentioned that speaks to the key of listening? It's: "a fool is thought wise if he keeps his mouth shut." And that became my philosophy. I just kept my mouth shut and listened all I could early on.

And with that simple approach I sold more medical systems

than anyone else in the company.

At that time, it was all really new technology. When I started out there was no computerization or automation in the medical office. And there was very little of it in hospitals. It was a new frontier.

As I wrote earlier, I originally started working in this field with the help of a recommendation from my sister's ex-boyfriend. That was my foot in the door—a relationship—but it wasn't the only piece of the puzzle. The other piece came from listening to a need and answering that need. What need, you may ask?

I got my start working with medical software from, of all things, writing parking tickets at my university.

I was prolific at writing parking tickets. It was my on-campus job, and at times I may have been the most hated guy on campus! Even so, I was very good at it, and I got great joy out of it. Ha.

But there was, at that time, only one computer on campus. The dean asked us, the whole staff, saying, "Look, we need to be able to enter these parking tickets into this new software system that they've written, this new program." Now, at the time, entering tickets so that they would attach to individual student accounts and go onto their bill automatically was a unique thought. The dean had a need. Nobody else stood up to do it, so I spoke up. I listened to what was needed instead of what I knew how to do, and took it upon myself to meet the need.

So, I started doing data input of all the parking tickets I and the other staff had written. And I got good at it. The program was so easy to use; it truly was just plain and simple data entry.

When I came out of college, it was this data entry position that gave me the qualifications I needed to step into the position of selling medical software. The relational link allowed me an initial connection to the job. But listening to a need and choosing to fill it gave me the experience I needed. And that's what I've been doing ever since. Listening didn't just give me my start in medical software, however.

When I got into this world of medical software, I realized I had a lot to learn and that I had to listen. That truth has carried over and served me well throughout these 34 plus years. The simple ability to listen instead of getting ahead of the client by jumping to conclusions about what they are asking for or what they need is vital. And there's good news: anyone can listen. Even more good news: anyone who can listen can succeed. I find that the people who run their mouths all the time or talk too much miss opportunities. If you're a good listener, however, you can figure out what your client needs and put together a solution they'll actually buy.

Again, this has so much to do with caring about what's important to them—not what's important to you. It's easy to think you've got this piece of software, this technology, this gizmo that you've got to go out and sell. No, that thinking won't help. You've got to figure out what the customer needs. Does your product actually fit their needs?

Being focused on the customer, not yourself, is the key to relational selling success. Listening is the key. And keeping your mouth shut is also a huge step to being able to hear what your prospect is trying to tell you. When you've listened, you get the chance to go back and say, "Do I understand correctly that this is what you're wanting?" Then you receive their affirmation in the process.

Listening is an art, I think. Both listening and understanding are things you must consciously develop. They take concentration. And in this world of distractions, with our phones and media flying all over the place, it's hard to listen. But the moment you step in front of that customer, they need to be 100% certain they've got your ears and eyes. You must listen. Let them know you're engaged, because only then can you be successful.

As a side note related to listening, let me share a quick story. Early in my career, I was with a senior IBM rep making a call to a clinic. We went in, made our way back to see the office manager, sat down, and had a conversation with her. It was a great conversation—lots of helpful information. At that time I was working on doing a great job at listening, or so I thought. After fifteen or twenty minutes, we finished up our talk with the office manager and walked back outside.

As soon as we got in the car and closed the doors, the senior rep turned to me and asked, "What was the name of the woman we just met with?" He continued, "What was she really looking for? What were her problems?" He quizzed me on and on and on. While I had been practicing listening, I was also trying to commit most of the information to memory at that time. It wasn't working. He emphatically told me, "Write it down!"

You simply cannot depend on your memory for all the details that you've got to keep up with in sales. I wasn't taking the proper notes I needed to take for me to understand and follow up in a timely manner. I couldn't memorize my way to addressing the issues that this clinic was having and present a solution that would help solve their problems.

When I began my career, most notetaking was done on an 8 ½" x 11" notepad and from there put into a binder for follow up. Now we have all kinds of note taking applications to help us. We also have the advent of all kinds of CRM systems out there to help us track and follow up with clients or prospects. These allow us to make projections and be accountable to our management, ourselves, and our clients.

For my notetaking needs, I love Evernote. I've been using it for the last several years, because it allows me to make notes on specific clients and days, continually building a database of knowledge about any given client's needs. What really makes it great for me is that it's searchable. It's a great tool whether on my laptop or phone—especially since the two stay synced up! For additional help keeping up with my prospects and specifically walking them through the sales process, I utilize an app called Pipedrive. It allows me and my team to tailor our sales process into simple steps that we then use to move someone from being interested to becoming a client.

You can get on the resources tab of our website to find out more applications we recommend. Until then, remember: listen well and write it down!

COMMON GROUNDS

by Ancil Lea, III

Human Relationships in Sales

BY WAYNE COX

Every job in the world involves salesmanship. And whether we like it or not, we receive training for sales from very different sources. In 1982, Jim Grant, the General Manager at KKYK-FM 104, shared an opportunity with me by investing a great amount of money in sales training. Snider Corporation owned this radio station, as well as another, and they both participated in a Sales Training Seminar. The basic concept was simple: discover the need of the customer and develop a plan to satisfy the need. I had been wrong in my focus. Instead of upselling the patron, I must determine and satisfy their needs.

My parents provided more pieces of my sales training. My father told me that people can tell when a salesperson is looking at them as a dollar sign. He advised me to listen to the customer, because he or she would tell me all about their business if I simply listened. And growing up, my mother would share idioms with me which, when applied, really worked. One of these was, "Those who hath friends must show themselves friendly." Applying this, I would truly befriend people who could help me see the decision makers within the different businesses I contacted.

Over time, I began to develop relationships with business owners. They were the people needing help and advice. The business owner knew how to be a plumber, a builder, a restaurateur, or even how to sell ladies ready-to-wear. They needed me to show them how to reach their potential consumers.

As a child I remember the only dairy products in our home came from Coleman Diary. Frequently, I would see a lady named Louise Luken on television as the spokesperson for Coleman Diary. One day, I reached out to Louise Luken in order to meet with Buddy Coleman. Of course, I engaged Louise in such a way that we both could meet with Buddy. We all became friends. I loved visiting with Buddy about his days as a Southwest Conference Referee. Together, we developed a plan for Coleman Diary to promote Home Delivery. We used Home Delivery at my home so why not help them grow their business through it? The Home Delivery campaign was so successful that Buddy received pressure from a national grocery chain. We maintained our friendship until Buddy sold the business to Turner Dairy.

At another time, I became acquainted with a gentleman named David Ruff. He was the CEO of Morrilton Packing Company. My initial meeting with David was in the mid-1980's, though we had both been students at the University of Arkansas in Fayetteville years earlier. At the time, there was another representative from the radio station working with David, however we still talked occasionally. Fast forward a few years with me: I had made inroads with David and his marketing manager when I was at KATV Channel 7. In March of 2014, I retired from KATV Channel 7 and began working for Dan

Fife Communications and Marketing in April of 2014. Dan had some clients already whom he had relationships with for a few years. I had two goals: to help the current clients grow their businesses and to expand the number of clients of Dan Fife Communications.

Since I already had a relationship with David Ruff, Dan Fife and I met with him one afternoon to discuss his business and the changes he had seen. Dan had experience working with Land 'O Frost, and David and I talked about the changes he and I had seen the marketing world. Dan Fife Communications and Marketing became the agency of record two weeks later.

Our goals were aligned. We aimed to help Petit Jean Meats become a front-of-the-mind smoked meats brand. The marketing plan worked, reaching two different target customers: the Meat Managers at the grocery stores and women who made the decisions from the home. I enjoyed working with David Ruff for years until his sudden death on January 31, 2018. I have been blessed to continue to work with David's son, Edward, who is carrying on the family line of owning and managing Petit Jean Meats. Edward and I have developed a relationship which helps us continue to work together toward continual success. These examples, as in all of my experience, show that relationships—real, human relationships—have been the key to success in sales and business.

COMMON GROUNDS
by Ancil Lea, III
COMMON GROUNDS
by Ancil Lea, III

Inquiring > Advocating

BY SPENCER JONES

People have different perceptions of what a salesperson should be, and how salespeople should act. Most people think that good salespeople are extroverts with pushy, domineering, and verbose tendencies. While this stereotype might be true for some, it's definitely not true for the great salespeople of the world. Success in selling doesn't come from beating people over the head with data or having a snappy response on the heels of every objection. You can convince them that you have the best mouse trap on the market, but if they don't trust you, feel listened to, and feel comfortable doing business with you, then it's game over.

When I was in my mid-20's, I attended the Milestone Leadership program that focused on leadership training and executive development. This multi-day retreat was full of workshops, team building activities, and all types of experiential learning projects. There were countless valuable lessons I took away from my time there, but the axiom that impressed upon me the most was simple: you should always be inquiring more than you're advocating. Being a fairly gregarious person myself, I had doubts about how applicable this was to me, or how realistic it was to practice this theory consistently. The more we discussed and applied this principle, it became evident that this simple maxim would have a huge impact on my ability to build rapport and influence people.

This past spring I was on a sales ride-along with one of our distributor reps in the midwest. She was prepping me as we headed to a hospital so I could understand who we were meeting with. We had a 30-minute meeting with a big-name director from a massive hospital, and she warned me that he could be terse and less than welcoming to sales reps. The three of us piled into a cramped room, and based on his initial demeanor and posture, I could immediately tell her characterization of him was dead on. I started the meeting by asking him about his role, his team, their focus, recent initiatives they'd undertaken, their most challenging problems, etc. I continued to probe about what they were using, if they were satisfied with it, what they'd like to improve on, etc. Throughout the discussion, we touched on complex clinical issues his team was facing and how they were dealing with them. We were at least 20 minutes into the 30-minute meeting before I even mentioned the device I was there to sell. One might question, "Why would you wait that long before talking about the device you're there to sell?"

Him voicing his problems allowed him to feel heard and instructed me as to which value proposition to focus on when I started my sales pitch. Having a clinical dialogue about his patients allowed me to establish clinical credibility and communicate targeted use cases for my device that addressed his patient's unique needs. As I took the time to inquire, investigate, and listen, it allowed him to gain trust, feel heard, and relax. An hour and fifteen minutes after the meeting started, we wrapped up and he walked us to the hospital entrance where we talked for another five minutes before parting ways. As we walked into the parking garage, the sales rep I was riding with remarked, "Well that was awesome, he never gives sales reps that much time."

People, including customers, treasure their own autonomy and have a fundamental need to be heard. They want to have their thoughts and grievances listened to and considered. As a salesperson, this is great news for you! Your customers have problems, and you have a solution that can hopefully solve at least one of those problems. This is why it's so important for salespeople to not only do more inquiring than advocating, but to do the inquiring first. If your product can help your customer in multiple ways, isn't it worth finding out what your customer's biggest problems are so you can emphasize the most relevant value proposition during your pitch? It's hard to fight the urge to start telling the customer all the amazing things about your product, especially when you're passionate about what you're selling. But good salespeople resist this urge and instead prioritize getting their customers talking. Whether it's personal or professional relationships, if you do more inquiring than advocating, the person on the other side will leave the conversation feeling more fulfilled, and you'll leave the conversation having gained more information for it.

The Pitch

BY ANCIL LEA

In one of the first jobs I had as a senior in high school, I learned things that I have applied through the rest of my career. I was working for a men's clothing store here in our city. Mr. and Mrs. Camp were the owners of this well-known, highly-thought-of men's fine clothing store. Though I'm still not sure how, I was able to sell myself there to get a position when they needed to hire. I found that I really enjoyed working there and had a knack for sales.

Even with my knack, however, I was fortunate that Mrs. Camp was a great teacher. One day she pulled me aside and said, "Look, when you lay out an outfit or, like, a sports jacket and pants and shirt and tie and belt and shoes," she said, "go ahead and pull out the stops. Pull out all kinds of different options and try them."

"Make a big presentation out of it," she encouraged. That advice really hit me and has stuck with me ever since—people want to see a big presentation. They want to see all their options. Mrs. Camp's guidance and the time she spent investing in me meant so much; it's stuck with me throughout all these years.

Fast-forward to just recently—I was working with a client, a software company. They asked me to give them pointers about their presentation. "Alright," I said, "you guys cut loose. Let's see it."

They instantly jumped into trying to show me how to use the software. They gave no background of who they were, who their clients were, or any information that would have been helpful to know before they jumped straight into the software. But jumping straight into the software made no sense. If I were a prospect, I would have had no frame of reference of where this product came from or how it was developed. You've got to be able to tell the story and make a big presentation.

And that's not all. Thinking back to my high school job, this company's presentation would be like handing someone who's just walked into the store a belt and explaining its fit before ever asking what they were looking for. Does the client you're presenting to actually need a belt? Knowing what someone needs takes relational work. Skipping this aspect of relational selling can waste a whole lot of time—both yours and theirs.

So what does all this mean? It means the pitch is so important. In baseball, you can't hit the ball unless somebody pitches it to you. And they have to pitch it in such a way that you can take a swing and hit it. Your pitch has to hit the mark. Fine-tuning your pitch is critical for sales success.

One of the best ways to get better at your pitch is to have outside eyes look at your whole presentation, much like what I was doing with this company, to give you honest feedback on how you're actually doing. My greatest teachers in getting better at my pitch include 1) failure and 2) really honing in on what the client is actually looking for. Remember, designing your pitch around what they're actually looking for or what they need is key to relational selling success.

Asking the right questions up front is critical to having a presentation, a pitch, that actually moves the prospect to becoming a client. You've got to get good at asking questions.

After doing this for over 35 years, I still find that I've got to stop and ask the questions before we're able to even begin. Sometimes I think I know what they need, but I could be completely wrong. And I've been completely wrong. But if I stop and ask the questions in order to get to the heart of their pain or what they really want, I can aim the presentation and/or pitch in a way that hits those pain points and meets their needs, so they'll want to go to the next step in the process. Your pitch, your presentation, is critical to moving them to the next step. And doing that well takes hard work up front to find out exactly what they're looking for.

As a bonus tip, remember that practice, practice, practice makes perfect in regards to your pitch! Once you get good at asking those questions, you can present your solution with confidence in the most favorable manner.

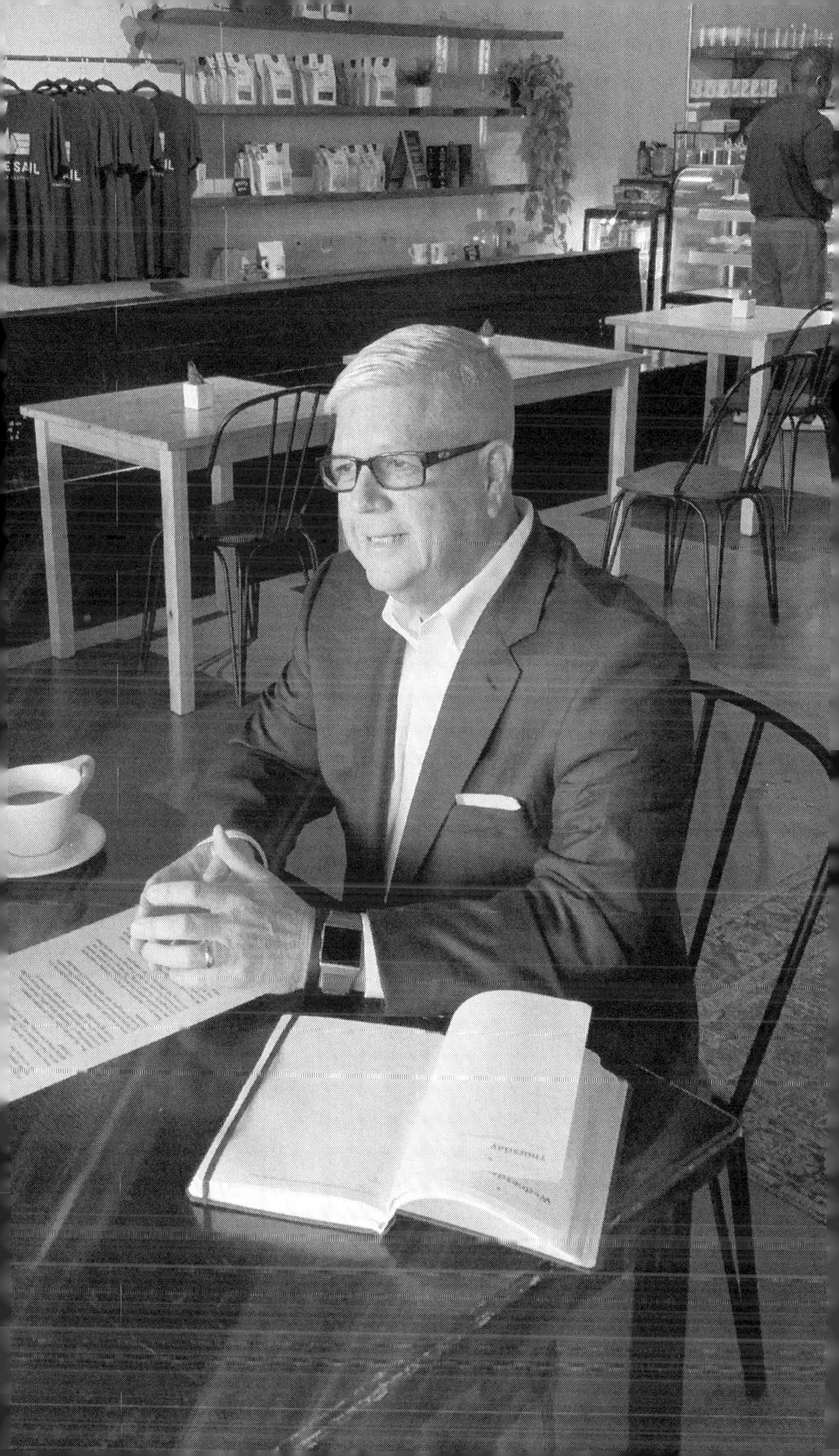

Insight & Client-Focus

BY BROOKE GARCIA

You may ask, what does Relational Selling mean to me and how does it impact my business?

Relational selling can mean many things to many different workers and user types. In my world relational selling means prioritizing the connection with the client above all other needs of the sale. In our world today, the relationship is key. Many Fortune 500 companies have now transitioned to a virtual workplace. In the virtual world we live, breathe, and work in today the art of relationship-building is more challenging than ever.

In society nearly two years ago, working America operated much differently. Most offices had individuals housed in cubicles or a tight-knit workplace setting. In more recent years the workplace economy shifted to a virtual work-from-home setting. Communicating, building, solving, and creating are now done via network at what we call the edge. The edge being defined as the forefront to everything connected to solving real needs and business problems.

You may ask, how does this impact the Art of Relational Selling? In my career I work at the forefront, assisting mainstream clients with global solutions and support. My business is built on the art of building trust with individuals across the globe from the standpoint of working at the edge remotely. It all comes down to three key areas my company focuses on heavily: *Hunger, Heart and Harmony*. I strive to live by these daily.

Hunger: Status quo? Not at Insight. Our insatiable desire to create new opportunities for clients and businesses across the world is apparent in everything we do. We are change agents, united in our passion to improve every day and deliver outstanding results for our clients.

Heart: seeking to have a positive impact on the lives of the people we serve by always putting our clients, partners, and teammates first.

Harmony: my company consists of many teammates on one global team. We invite perspective, and we celebrate each other's unique contributions as we work together. Our team is diverse; we value inclusivity and create meaningful connections so that we can reach success together.

The explosion of data and technology has created noise for users across the globe. That drives the importance of finding a 'Common Ground' with your clientele. Gaining their trust is not only built on a framework of numbers, pricing, and percentages. It's also built with the root of establishing a commonality.

An example of this commonality, I had a client who wanted a complete hands-off experience for solutioning, delivering and scaling products around the globe for their company. They requested both hardware and software alongside services to support the business needs and security measures their company required.

My company is a large competitor on the global scale, with over 6,000+ hardware, software, and cloud partners. We are located in 18 countries across the globe with over 11,000+ teammates worldwide. For this client, our scale won the business but also threatened the relationship. The client wanted what many prefer, a one-stop shop or as we call it "one back to pat" for all their requests, concerns, and escalations worldwide. Because the client is in many countries, a larger client would require working with numerous contacts for each country they are located in. This client preferred to only have one single point of contact for all their business needs.

We activated relational selling internally as a team. We built out an internal service offering where a client could utilize what we refer to as a Global Project Manager. This person's role would be to live, eat and breathe the client's needs. They would have a laser focus on relationship building with all Insight global locations. They prioritize client requirements and ensure SLAs and expectations are met. Upon implementing this resource for the client to expand globally with our company, we were able to meet their needs, adapt to their environmental request and maintain a successful, profitable business relationship.

In the business world it's about adding value to a client, putting their needs first and setting realistic expectations up front. The Art of Relational Selling will always be the framework to the business world we live in today.

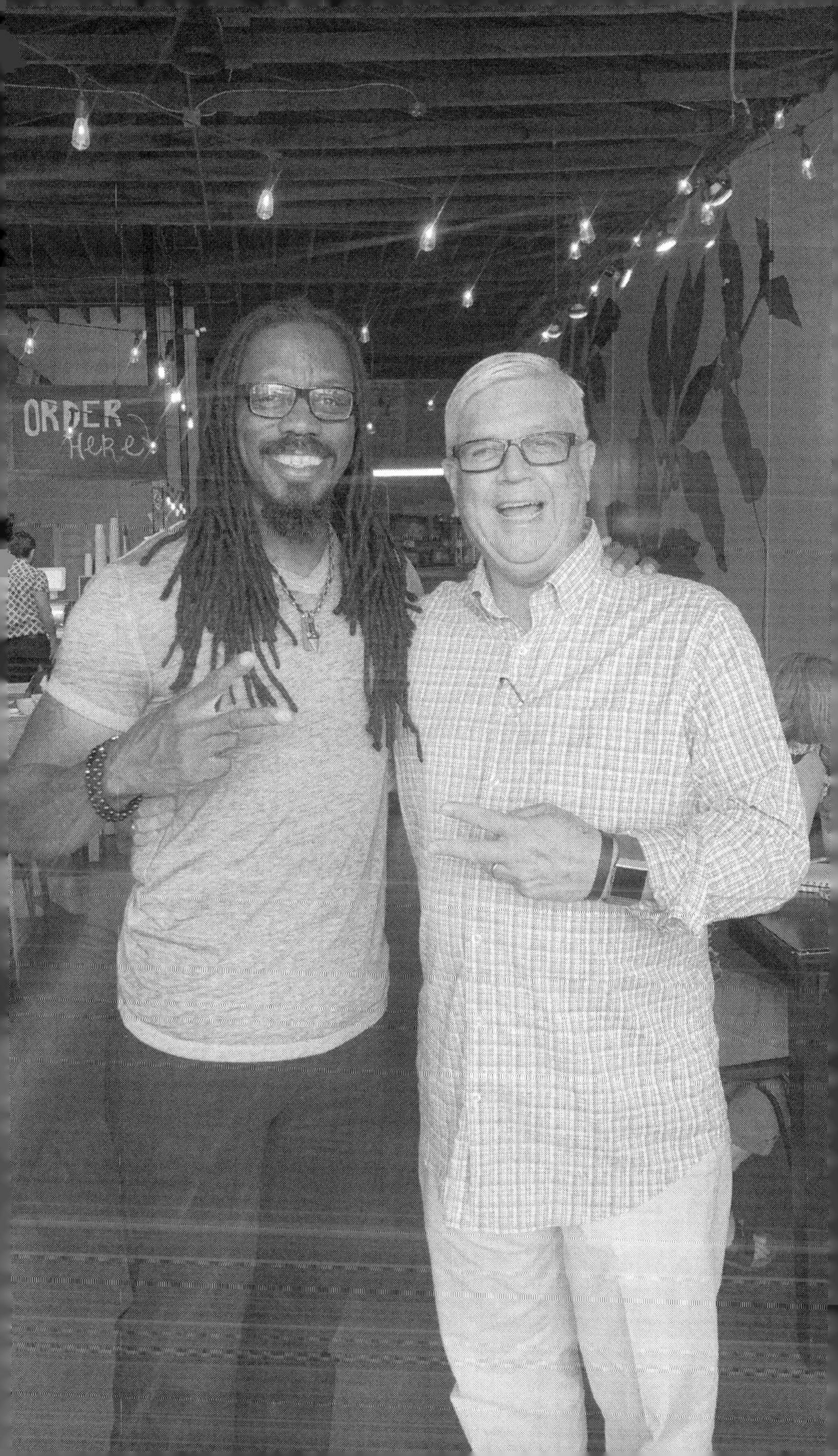
ORDER
Here

Validation

BY ANCIL LEA

Several months ago I was sitting in a conference with a business coach of ours. Our coach happens to be part of a venture capital group that has made several investments in health tech companies. For one of these companies she was asked to accompany them to a sales call for a very large hospital system. During the sales call, this health tech company presented to the CEO and the CEO's team of about five or six people.

The presentation went great, and they all really loved the product, especially the CEO. However, while they were looking at the product, several of the team members went on their phones and started researching both the product and the health tech company behind the product. They brought to the attention of everyone during the presentation that there was no proof or testimonials or even a really good website for this product. They were looking for validation that this product had been successful somewhere else, that the product actually worked, that it was real...you get the picture. They did the research while they were there in the meeting, and they did not find what they were looking for. What happened was a huge setback to the whole sales process, because now the health tech company had to validate their product in another way.

Just because you have a great product doesn't mean that you won't have to lay the foundation blocks—your validation—so that you can sell and be successful. In her closing remarks, as my coach made her point in the conference, she turned toward me and said, "That's why you need Ancil and his group!"

Validation is huge. Since I began working in healthcare over 34 years ago there have been many changes in how the rules operate and the best way to get new clients. Several things, however, remain as true today as they have ever been in regards to selling HealthTech and Medical Software. Let's call them the building blocks or foundational pieces that you need to have in place to be successful at selling your solution.

One of the big building blocks you've got to have in place when you're out selling is proof or validation that your solution works. It's not enough to have a nice website—you must have relational proof of your product or solution. Today people look at your LinkedIn account, your website, and any other media they can in order to find out if this solution is for real, to decide if they should spend their time on you, and to discern if your solution is a fit for their organization.

This is why having successful initial installs or beta sites are so, so helpful in getting sales generated. Having people say how much they love your product and what it's done for them gives others who review this validation confidence that your solution actually works, that they can invest in it, and that it would work for them as well. In my experience, having video customer testimonials are powerful; they really do a lot of the work for you! The reason? They show trust between you and other clients. These testimonials are a form of relationship building for new clients; they show that you can be trusted and that you have relationships with other companies that are going well. As I've been pointing out: relationships are key!

So, if you have your first few clients up and going on your solution, you must leverage these for all they're worth. Create sound blog posts, great white papers, and confidence-building testimonial videos about your solution. Build reasons for people to trust you. Leverage these early successes for future sales.

And, as a start up, if you don't have any beta sites or development partners yet—you have got to go out and get these 'early adopters' to be able to get your sales really going. I have found that giving incentives to be your development partners through discounted pricing (even free for a period of time) helps to get them on board. There are multiple ways to approach not having your solution out there yet and getting these early adopters. Keep in mind that without these, selling will remain very difficult.

Getting your product or solution out there with 'validation' is pivotal. What's as important though? Validation of who you are and your own personal brand. People are not only looking for validation about the product or solution you're trying to sell, they're looking for validation and proof about you as well. You can't sell anything if people don't believe in you!

Let me also say that your personal brand has to be in place these days for you to be taken seriously. Most C-suite execs are going to check you out before you walk in the door or even while you're on a zoom or phone call. The first place they're going to look to validate who you are and your experience is LinkedIn. Your LinkedIn profile is so important because it is not only your résumé with all of your experience, testimonials, and endorsements—it's part of your personal brand and connections. People see your endorsements and testimonials about you as well as the kind of content you post.

So, developing your LinkedIn presence and your connections is a big part of validating who you are. Be sure to connect with your prospects on LinkedIn by the time you walk in the door or do a zoom meeting to show them your solution. And be sure you've already done your homework about them and their team to see if there's any additional connections that you share with them. Remember, every bit of this builds trust between you and your potential client.

Let me say again: video testimonials are a powerful source of social proof and validation whether it's about you or about your product or solution. It's good to have video interviews of you on your profile, too. Through all these videos, people can check you out to see if you are for real. Trust me, people will take time to watch a two minute video you put out!

So let's recap—you need social, or relational, proof to give your prospects 'validation' or confidence to move forward working with you and your solution.

Develop your LinkedIn profile for you and, by association, your product.

Have your web presence up to date and filled with customer testimonials and product information.

Make sure your branding is consistent on all your media—LinkedIn, website, and any other social media you use.

I recommend you get someone from outside to review and grade you on these items.

Being Known and Trusted

BY CLAY MCKINNEY

My first sales role was for a Fortune 500 company as a Financial Advisor. They provided the best training in the industry. I learned how to block my time, what questions to ask, how to ask for the business, etc. The training was much needed, especially for a recent college graduate with only a couple of years of working experience. I quickly learned that even if I did and said all the right things, I still might not make the sale. But if I had an existing relationship or was able to build a relationship throughout the sales process, my chances of making the sale went up dramatically. The most important lesson learned was this: People do business with people they know and trust.

Fast forward to my current role as President of Hatcher Capital Investments (HCI), and the saying above still rings true. People do business with people they know and trust. I met with a prospect shortly after I started with HCI at the end of 2018. In that initial meeting, I did and said all the right things. I showed them how we partner with our clients, the cost savings they would have if they made the switch, and even sent a handwritten thank you note after the meeting. I thought it was a home run. But unfortunately, I didn't win the business. They had been working with the same advisor for the last ten years. They told me I could check in once or twice a year on them but decided to not make any changes at the time. Instead of having my feelings hurt, I continued to check in twice a year just like they requested. I shared market updates, sent birthday and holiday cards, went to lunch, and just built a relationship. Three years later, when the prospect was considering making a change again, I was the first person they called. And this time, the meeting actually was a home run.

People do business with people they know and trust. It's that simple. Do what you say you are going to do. Follow through on your promises. Treat others how you would want to be treated. If you are organized, driven, and talented, you'll probably experience some success from the start. But if you can build trust and relationships with your clients, then you'll never have to "sell" again.

Building Trust in the Basics

BY DAVID HOUSE

Selling starts with relationship, and every relationship is based on trust. Therefore, successful selling is based on trust as well.

The fundamental way you develop trust in a relationship is by being true to your word and looking out after the other person's best interest as well as your own. The first thing it takes to be successful with relational selling is to believe in the product you're selling, and believe that the product will—and that you can and will— deliver what you promise. Realize that anything you commit is a promise. You may call it a commitment. Your customer calls it a promise. So, you have to trust in the product you're selling and its ability to deliver.

The other thing is that your potential customer has to have a legitimate need. I can't tell you how many times over the years I have had people call on me with a solution looking for a problem. Often, folks don't even know what problem their solution will solve. Say a salesman comes to me and says, "Hey, I'm selling X." And I reply,

"Well, what problem does your solution solve?" I can tell you, I've met many salespeople who don't have a clue. If you don't know what problem you're trying to solve, then you need to do your homework and figure that out. Don't be a solution looking for a problem.

The other thing is, along the same lines, you really have to understand, does the customer you're targeting truly have the problem that your solution answers? Say you're selling the best hairbrush in the world. It's made of the right material, has the right weight, the right fiber strength, everything. It's truly the superior product. But if I am bald, I do not need your product. And if you try to sell me the hairbrush, then we're going to have a major disconnect.

So, have a product that you believe in. Understand what problems your products solve. Then, make sure your prospective customer actually has a need for your product. If they don't, you're really doing them a disservice.

The other thing I would say to keep in mind is that I as a potential customer am looking for a reference. The reason I want a reference is because it tells me someone else has actually successfully bought your product. You have delivered your product, and it has met their needs. So with every sale that you have, you should make sure that your customer is pleased enough with your product that you can reference them. And if they're not, then you really are going to have a problem, number one, reselling to that customer and, number two, being able to use that customer for a reference, which will definitely impact your future sales.

From there, after you've started out with a potential customer and done those fundamental things, the way you build trust is really pretty simple: you under-commit and over-deliver. Make sure that if you're going to call a guy at 10 o'clock on Tuesday, you call him at 10 o'clock on Tuesday. Make sure that if you tell them you're going to have them a proposal by a week from tomorrow, they have a proposal by a week from tomorrow. And if you make a proposal and deliver a contract to them, the contract should have the exact terms and conditions that you've already discussed.

Each one of these is an opportunity to either build or destroy trust. Be consistent even in the little things, so that you match your actions with what you've said. That's how you build trust.

Now, the tricky thing with trust is it's very difficult to build and very easy to lose. You need to be very careful not to do things that would undermine trust. Let me give you an example: I worked for IBM for 10 years, and one of the things we were taught to do is to call high in the organization. So we did that. At least once a year I would call on the CEO of an organization, even when the CEO didn't sign the agreements. Usually a guy over in the technology area, maybe the VP or Director of Information Systems, would sign. They were the guys I was actually doing day-to-day business with.

So if I was going to call on their CEO, I first of all made them aware. If appropriate, I would even invite them to go with me. And if it wasn't appropriate or if I just ran into their CEO unexpectedly, I would always follow up with my main contact and say, "Hey, by the way, I called on so-and-so, and this is what we discussed; I just wanted to make you aware."

This is the way you begin to build trust so that folks don't feel like you're going around them or not looking out after their best interest. These are all pieces of building trust. Most of it comes down to just being courteous, being a person of your word, and living up to what you've committed.

Beyond that, owning your own mistakes is a huge opportunity to value the relationship and build trust. I'll tell you a quick story. When I was a young sales guy—24 or 25 years old—I was working for IBM. I had a young family; and I needed to make a living. A situation arose where I was working on a deal, and the way it worked was such that I had a bonus coming if I closed the deal by June the 30th. So I was very focused on closing this deal by that date. And so, on June the 29th, I called the customer. He says, "Yeah, I'm ready to do it. Come over and pick up your check." So, I went over and picked up my check to take it back and turn it in. I'm set to get a bonus for having closed this business by the end of the month.

Well, within a few hours of the beginning of the next month, July the 1st, the customer calls me and says, "David, by the way, I was thinking about this, and I think that if I actually paid one more day's rent I would get the benefit for a full month because I believe accruals for my rent actually are applied on the first of the month. So, if I paid one more day's rent, then I would actually save money by doing this on the first of the month versus doing it on the last day of the month." I sat there for a minute, and I said, "Well, I'll tell you what, let me think about that."

I hung up the phone, and I started thinking about it. And I thought, you know what, he is exactly right. It's a better deal for him if he waits one day. So, I picked up the phone, and I called him. I said, "Hey, you are exactly right. I am going to go and retrieve that check. You can write me another check tomorrow, July the 1st, and it will save you X-thousands of dollars."

And I added this, and this was the truth: "By the way, you should have never had to tell me this. I should have been looking out after your best interests and not mine. Honestly, I had a bonus I was going to get if I did this by the end of the month, and I should have run the bases more thoroughly. Had I done that, I would have discovered this, and I would have been telling you about this versus you telling me this. So, I want to admit to you that I was not looking out after your company's best interest. I want to apologize to you for that. And I want to tell you, in the future I won't make this same mistake."

He replied, "Hey, David, I get it. And I appreciate that. And I appreciate you being honest with me." So, I hung up the phone and went to pick up the check. I did not get my bonus, but here's the deal: I kept that customer for years. He always bought from me, and he never questioned me. Even though he had to point out the right way to do the transaction, because I came clean and I told him the truth, he could trust me. And he knew that if I recommended something for him, I had done the research and was working in his best interest.

Here's the thing you have to remember: trust is based on you working for your customer's best interest and not just yours. Sometimes that is very difficult to do, especially when you can get blinded by your own quota and your own bills. But I can say honestly, if you keep your customer in mind, your customer will not only always win—you will always win. Maybe not in the short term, but definitely in the long term.

Trust within relational selling is as simple as you doing the things that you say you're going to do in the timeframe that you say you're going to do it and always looking out after their best interests instead of just your own.

I used to say to customers all the time who would come to me who were really interested in making money, "Look, here's the deal: if you're in the software or hardware or really any business, if your whole goal is to make money, you will fail. If your whole goal is to make a great product, you will make money. And you will make money not only today, but you'll make money tomorrow." Part of making a great product is making sure your product meets my needs, that I have the need, and then delivering it under the terms and conditions in the timeframe you've committed. You begin a pattern of that and I guarantee you, you will make plenty of money and be very successful.

How Relationships Broke the Internet

BY DARREN HUCKEY

In March of 2022, my favorite fantasy author, Brandon Sanderson, made history. It all started when he posted a very brief YouTube video that struck fear into his fanbase at the beginning of March. Appearing very disheveled in the video, he began by saying, "I have been lying to you, and it is time for me to admit the truth." He said that he had not been forthright with his fans over the last couple of years and needed to come clean about some things. Fans like myself were immediately concerned, thinking the worst. What had happened? Was he having health issues? Family problems? Some kind of scandal, heaven forbid? Thirty days later he had not only "broken" the internet, but completed the highest-funded Kickstarter campaign of all time. What happened? Let's take a look.

First, who is Brandon Sanderson? He is a New York Times Best Seller author who writes epic fantasy and science fiction. He has published more than two dozen books to date, with many more scheduled. He has built an epic fantasy equivalent of the Marvel Universe, called the Cosmere, that many of his books are tied into. He has multiple series of books, with the most popular being Mistborn and The Stormlight Archive.

To many people, Sanderson seems like an overnight success because of being chosen to finish the wildly popular Wheel of Time series after author Robert Jordan died. This instantly launched him into the limelight, setting him on a path of success. But his success didn't start there. It started when he wrote thirteen full-length novel manuscripts before ever being published. He put in the hard work required to become an author before ever getting paid to do so. The same is true for how Sanderson created the devoted fanbase that has launched him into superstar status. Sanderson has been paying his dues for nearly two decades by keeping a pulse on his fans and interacting with them on a regularity that is almost unprecedented. Not only does he display his writing progress and release sneak previews for various projects on his website, but he also posts regular updates on Reddit and Twitter, posts a weekly video progress update, and a two-hour live stream where he signs books while he answers fan questions as well. He constantly wears a smile and is equally respectful to everyone. Not only is he a fantastic writer, he's a guy you can't help but like.

What was so spectacular about Sanderson's video that launched him into another level of stardom after he published his March video update? In this video he gave a full "confession" of his faults that began by stating how different people handle stress differently and that the last two years of the pandemic had taken its toll on everyone, including him. And then he let it out... He had dealt with the stress by... writing a book without telling anyone. Well, actually, two books. No, three. Sorry... when the dust finally settled, he revealed he had written a total of FIVE books, four of which were full-length novels—IN ADDITION TO the nearly half a dozen books he writes every year. And all without his staff or his fans ever knowing about it. Yes, Sanderson fans already knew he was prolific, but this blew everyone's mind.

And not only did he just reveal that he had written these books, but he had come up with a way to quickly get the four novels into the hands of his fans. He had created a Kickstarter campaign to self-publish them, rather than undergoing the long process of going through his publisher. He scheduled them to be released, one novel per quarter, in 2023. Within the first half-hour of the campaign, his $1 million goal had been surpassed and the campaign closed thirty days later at $41.7 million—more than DOUBLE the former highest Kickstarter campaign ever. This totally caught Sanderson by surprise. Midway through the campaign, he sent out an email thanking his backers that said, "I'm supposed to WRITE fantasy worlds—not live in them."

Why was Sanderson's campaign so successful? Was it simply clever marketing tactics as some may believe? This level of success doesn't come as the result of a mere marketing ploy. Success on this level only comes with a trusted relationship between an author and his fans. Because of his past achievements and communication, his fans knew that Sanderson—unlike many currently popular authors—could deliver on his promises. And the numbers of his Kickstarter campaign back that up, with more than 185,000 people pledging to back his campaign. Before the campaign ever began, Sanderson had spent years building trust and rapport with his fan base, his customers. One of the things I didn't mention earlier is that Sanderson is also adjunct faculty at Brigham Young University, where he teaches a creative writing course once per year, another example of giving back to the community who helped develop him as a writer. He also makes these classes available online for free. One of the reasons Sanderson fans like him so much is because he does things like this, giving back to his fans whenever possible.

To sum up what I have called the "Sanderson Effect," Brandon Sanderson is someone who knows that you can't go for the "ask" without first giving and building a relationship in which your customers can see that you're not just after their wallet. They need to see who you are as a person in addition to your passion for what you do. Your customers need to be on the receiving end of the relationship before they will be willing to be on the giving end. And not only do they need to know that your relationship with them doesn't start and end with the sale, they need to see you consistently delivering on your promises. Unfortunately, over-commitment and under-delivery plagues many who are striving for success. Based on Sanderson's success, my recommendation is to start slow, be consistent, and invest long term in your client-base by giving away content and interacting with your customers. As we can see from this example, the rewards are worth the wait. Thanks, Brandon, for the great example you have given to us all.

Secret Sauce

BY ANCIL LEA

When you've got a product to sell and a quota to reach, it's easy to become overwhelmed and discouraged. But if you take it a little bite at a time, you can achieve your goals. It all comes down to knowing your aim, being willing to work at daily tasks, and staying aware of your next steps.

Early in my career, I had to put together a plan for my IBM general manager and present it to him on how I was going to reach my quota for the year. "A plan for the whole year?" I thought! "How in the world am I going to do this?"

And they didn't want broad goals - they wanted specifics, such as when exactly a particular system would be sold. It was like looking into a crystal ball and just hoping to see the plan unfold. This magic plan had to include everything—marketing events that you'd use to gain prospects, developing those prospects through the entire sales cycle, and finally getting them to actually sign a contract thereby becoming clients.

That was an incredibly daunting process. So, I struggled to put it together.

I mean, I spent hours thinking through all the pieces and putting it all down on paper. Keep in mind, back then there was no PowerPoint. Presentations were done on overhead projectors. I still remember having to design and print out overhead slides to share! But I did my presentation. For fun I added a little levity, a little humor in there as well, and presented it all to the manager.

Throughout that year I will never forget how amazing it was to watch certain dates and events roll out just as I'd planned them. I was making these projections, reports, and plans in January for the entire year ahead and pitching them to my manager. It was remarkable to actually see them unfold as I'd predicted.

I still remember one of the most shocking sales that came to fruition. I had projected a certain system would be purchased by a particular large clinic in November. Now, these guys hadn't bought anything in years—yet I projected they would buy a system in November. I freely admit it was a purely hopeful projection—I was just pie in the sky.

Low and behold, of all things, they bought the system in November, exactly when I had projected them to. By that point in the year, I was just sitting there wondering how that happened. Magic, perhaps? But no, it wasn't magic. Perhaps there were subliminal things going on internally with me to make it happen?

There are always aspects along the way you cannot control. But my takeaways from this first yearly plan was that 1) I had an aim, and 2) I pursued daily activity toward that aim. I aimed toward hitting my quota, and I formed a plan on how I was going to get there. Beyond that, I focused on the daily motions I needed to do to reach that quota. It was all about the activities I did every hour of every day.

A "magic" formula that one senior IBM rep taught me was:

calls + demos = sales. Taking that into today's vernacular, calls can really mean all activity. Activity alongside demonstrations is what leads to sales. It's that simple. If you keep it simple, you will achieve your goals.

So what activity should you be doing on a daily basis? This is really where the magic is. For starters, you need to be generating LinkedIn posts. You need to be emailing people. You need to be direct messaging or sending texts. You need to be contacting people on a daily basis, either to set up your demonstrations or follow up to see what the next step is.

This is one of the things that a manager taught me early on. She would require a report every week documenting all the activity or demonstrations I'd done the week before. Her constant mantra, which she drilled into me, was always: what's the next step? I learned to go into every meeting thinking about how to move someone to the next step. It was one thing to tell my branch or marketing or sales manager about a meeting. It was another to begin focusing on how to move this thing down the road.

And it's all about the next step. While you're having a meeting or demonstration, you have to come out of that demonstration knowing what the next step is. Is the next step a proposal? Is the next step for them to talk to a reference? Is the next step, and so on—it could be anything or even multiple things. The key is having a next step and keeping them stepping forward until there is a decision. The decision may be, "Hey, I'm going to buy this thing," or it may be that they've decided to wait or have decided it's a no. But you have to get to that fork in the road. Only there can you get people signing contracts. And to get to that place, you must have an aim and consistent, daily activity. Those two things are what matters in the end.

Stories from the Field

BY JASON SWEET

I had the wonderful privilege of growing up in a family of entrepreneurs. My unique upbringing has shaped the way I view relationships and ultimately how I interact with others. My grandfather grew up without a father (he'd lost his dad at six years old to mustard gas in WW1), but he had a passion for the outdoors. He married into a wealthy Italian immigrant family. He decided at a very young age he would weave his career into his passion. He created a company called Decoys Unlimited and made decorative and hunting decoys. He was a very skilled woodworker and painter and was fortunate to win the 1966 World Decoy Carving Championship. In 1976, with his older brother's encouragement, my grandparents decided to leave everything they had created in Pennsylvania to move out west to Idaho and open a small hunting, fishing, and gunsmithing shop.

My childhood was everything a boy could dream of. I owned a horse named Rufus that my grandfather gave me for my eighth birthday and spent most of my free time outside enjoying God's creation. I was fortunate to witness the inner workings of a family business. My father is one of the best salesmen I have ever been around. He frequently would have the traveling sales rep stay at our house and multiple times we vacationed with some of these families who had become great friends.

The lesson I learned from my dad is that the relationship is the end goal, not profit margin, money, etc.

Growing up I was very close to my grandparents. We lived on ten acres together and shared a driveway. Our favorite activity to enjoy together was fishing. Our fishing trips took us to Alaska, Montana, Idaho, Nevada, and Pennsylvania. We had this contest where we would wager each trip, $1 for the first fish, $1 for the biggest fish, and $1 for the most fish. What I have learned from this lesson is that we never forget our first deal, our biggest deal, and the deal that required the most effort to win.

First Sales Win - I was a new recruiter, and we have an exclusive project with a large healthcare system located in NE Florida. Part of our exclusive program included hiring temp/contract resources, but the majority of our project was finding full-time employees who would most likely have to relocate from out of state. I was working on a business analyst position and came across a great candidate located in Austin, Texas. We spoke briefly on the phone, and I was impressed with his experience, professionalism, and career aspirations. The biggest challenge I faced with him was his years of experience. The role required five years of experience and he only had two. After the call I wrote him a handwritten thank you note for his time. A week later I received a LinkedIn message from him at the exact moment my account manager was at my desk speaking to me about the position. The timing was perfect, and she wanted to speak with the candidate. He was my first placement and made a huge impact on the health system. To this day, he's still a good friend.

Summer of 2018 I was flying from Little Rock, Arkansas to Jacksonville, Florida. My flight was delayed due to weather, and I was stuck in a small airport with only one option to eat with my voucher. Quiznos subs was the only food available because of renovations happening. Seating was very limited, and a nice passenger invited me to sit with him to eat our sandwiches. We quickly connected on family, faith, and work. I explained my role and the core values of the current company I was working with. The gentleman I was speaking with shared with me about his niece who was a recent college graduate, 4.0 college athlete with an MBA and struggling to find a meaningful job. He mentioned she was located in Central Florida. I told him that I would love to speak with her. Fast forward four years to right now; she is currently the leading producer at the company I helped her get a job at. She is making incredible money and having a huge impact in her current organization.

In the winter of 2022, I started a new role with a new company I had been tracking since 2014. During my first month with the company I was speaking with the most senior sales person at the organization about sales strategies. We were discussing how important integrity, relationships, and being memorable was. He asked me if I had ever heard of an auto repair chain in North Florida called RPM Automotive. I shared that I had heard of them and actually had taken all of my vehicles to RPM. I knew this auto repair store was not the cheapest in town but they provided honest, high quality work. The most memorable part of RPM was the front desk person named Bobby. He knew everyone by name and was always willing to make small talk. Oftentimes Bobby would call and explain the repair options and how they were trying to help with options between OEM parts or imports. As I was talking to this senior sales guy at my current organization about the importance of relationships, he said the gentleman at the front desk, Bobby, was his father; he just retired last year.

Lessons Learned:
- Be memorable
- Do the little things, like hand-written thank you notes
- Focus on great people

Power in Collaboration

BY ANCIL LEA

While trying to grow your business and relationships, I find that collaborating with others is a powerful force for accomplishing that end. Working with people who can send you new contacts or prospects which might turn into business is extremely valuable, particularly if they've developed trust with these contacts already. It becomes a transfer of trust. Someone this prospect trusts reaches out and refers them to you, saying, "Hey, Ancil can help you with this type of software solution," thereby communicating, "As you trust me, trust Ancil with this need of yours."

It is so important that we collaborate. And collaboration is not a one-way street. What I mean by that is that the person who is helping you—a consultant, a CPA firm, a software company executive, etc.—they should win as well. Sometimes winning looks like making sure their client, friend, the person they're referring to you succeeds in getting the solution from you that they really need. As someone who this referral partner has trusted enough to share their contact with, make sure that you take great care to treat their contact well, to know them, and to know their needs in order to address those needs well.

In collaborating, again, you want the person who sent you the referral to win as well. One way, as I stated already, is to help the person they sent your way reach success. That's one way. The second way is to actually send them business back, showing that you're looking for opportunities to connect them with, whether it be one of your current clients or maybe a great prospect you run across and realize the prospect could really use what they do. And you set up an introduction. You do an e-introduction via email. Or, like what I did just this week, you actually set up a meeting and bring these two together over a meal or a cup of coffee just to make an introduction. Find a way to hand off the prospect to the person who can help them.

Like I said, this week I was set to have lunch with a large-hospital-system executive, and I had a friend who had a health-tech solution that they had developed who happened to be in town as well. I initially asked to meet with my health-tech buddy separately, but the only time he had was during lunch. So, I just reached out to the hospital executive and said, "hey, is it okay if I bring my friend along?" He said, sure. I brought my friend into the meeting and was able to introduce him and his solution. And, you know, something may happen there for them both.

Making these connections is powerful and very fulfilling. It all goes back to the mindset of—to get, you've got to give. And if you will give first to help others reach their objectives and goals, it will come back to you in a great multiple of blessings in the way of friends and new business. It is a powerful thing to give. I use this collaboration model because I've had so many people bless me through sending leads and business my way. And I want to return the favor. This is a relationship scenario that will keep on multiplying if you nurture it correctly and collaborate so that what you're doing is truly a win-win situation for all parties.

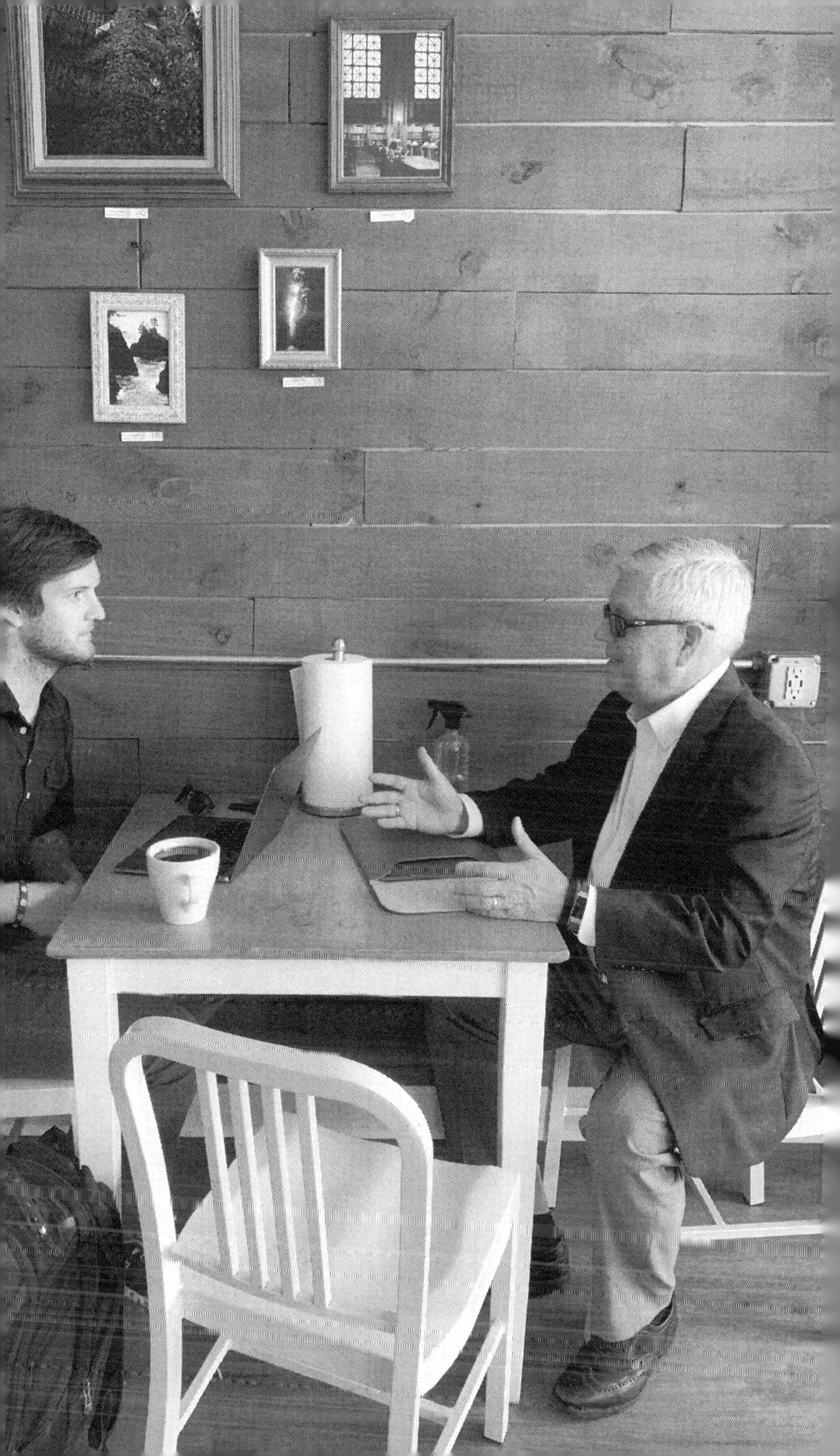

One more call

BY GEOFFREY BEECHER

I am the son of a Naval Aviator. He was also a physician. World War ll pilot. Brave guy. He worked hard his whole life. And, as an aside, it was mother that we feared the most. So did he.

I was about thirteen years old when my parents had their "fill" of my antics, and the summer was just starting. I was the sixth child of seven, and I was driving them crazy. Running around the city and creating mischief was my modus operandi. My older sister had just gotten married and moved to start her new life on a 1200 acre farm in Southwest Virginia, the heart of Appalachia and as beautiful a place as anywhere on earth. And that's where my parents sent me... out in the middle of nowhere - to work the farm, and maybe learn something, and stay out of trouble.

My first experience as a "farm hand" was to put up hay. Then move the cattle to another pasture. I had no idea what I was doing. But I was under the guidance of a farm hand named Lonnie. His southern accent mesmerized me, as did his work ethic. He was a strong man, and I was just a boy, and I was getting a workout in the hot Virginia sun. The mountains, the occasional breeze and the honeysuckle tricked my mind into thinking this was heaven, as we know from the song, "it's almost heaven."

It was a working farm with cattle, a couple of horses, and a field of tobacco and sorghum. I generally didn't know what I would be doing when I rose early in the morning. It was maybe my second or third day, when I was told the tobacco crop needed attention; it was being overrun by weeds. Back then, I guess there weren't automated systems, like "weed whackers," or at least we didn't have them. I was given a sickle and a machete. So the plan was for Lonnie and me to clear the field of weeds, row by row exposing the crop to the much needed sun.

One More Row

Lonnie and I attacked the field, and knocked down the towering, infiltrating weeds. It was hot, and we worked hard. I wasn't afraid of the work, I was, however, afraid of the Eastern Diamondback Rattler that Lonnie informed me of. I couldn't stop thinking about rattlesnakes.

We moved through the rows slowly. I thought it might take days to clear this field. At the end of each row, I thought we might "call it a day," because Lonnie had said on the previous row, "just one more row, Jethro." That was the theme: "one more row." And at the end of the next row? "How about one more row?" This went on until the sun started to sink behind Bear Creek Mountain when, finally, we finished the last row! The field was clear, and the tobacco was already looking healthier.

I would finish the summer on the farm and head back home with a love of the mountains, the front porch, and Chet Atkins.

20 Years Later

I was hired by Ethicon Endo Surgery to manage the Southwest Virginia market. These were "my old stomping grounds" as a "farm hand." The company, a division of Johnson and Johnson, had a full line of instruments for open and minimally invasive surgery. I couldn't have been more proud to be on this team. This was a time when technology made a huge leap forward, and I was in the middle of this disruptive transition. Ostensibly, I was in surgery with our instruments everyday, backed by a company "Credo" that we served the patients, the physicians, and the nurses. That's what we do. If we take care of these, everything is taken care of.

One More Call

One day, I was in a case that started at 7:30am and lasted until around 2pm. A long day for everyone. I had about an hour and a half drive home. While I was changing in the locker room, I thought, "I could get home in time to throw the ball with my son, or see my daughters at gymnastics practice." That was my original thought. As I got to my car, however, that thought changed.

On the drive home, I would be going right by a hospital and a surgeon who I couldn't convert to our system. And as I was driving, I was near the farm. I could hear Lonnie's words..."one more row, one more row." And I said it out loud: "one more row," which meant "one more call."

When I pulled into the hospital, I armed myself with brochures and my sterile instrument bag and headed to the OR to speak with the Director about a new device. It was a cold call (at a time when you could actually make one).

As I entered the unit, a circulating nurse saw me (she knew who I was). She disappeared into room three, and then re-emerged.

She was walking fast. There was something urgent going on in room three.

I was told to put on a "white jumpsuit" over my street clothes, mask up, and follow her in.

I had been in a lot of surgical cases, but this one was different. There was a lot of blood in the surgical field. An inordinate amount. I thought the patient might be a trauma or gunshot victim? No.

It was a low anterior resection, a bowel cancer case. The (competitive) internal stapler had misfired, and the surgeon was battling to achieve hemostasis. I recall the scenario: a male low anterior resection followed by anastomosis. Removal of the lower aspect (rectum) and then reconnected to the colon. But the failed staple line was changing things rapidly. The surgeon couldn't get beyond the failed staple line, the narrow male pelvis was limiting, there was no room. A permanent colostomy was coming into view for this patient. The surgeon asked me after showing me the situation if "we had a stapler that could get beyond the bleeding line?"

We had just released a new stapler, with a malleable head, narrower, more maneuverable. I was hopeful. We opened the new device and positioned it in the patient, and fired it! My heart rate was elevated, big time.

And it worked! The reattachment (anastomosis) was complete, the colostomy was avoided.

The only thought I had on my way home was how happy I was about the outcome. Did I earn the surgeon's business?

No.

I earned something much greater than I could've ever imagined that day: the satisfaction of making a difference, and the realization of how much I love my job.

Make the effort. Make one more call. One more row. Make a difference. As my dad would say, "push, you never know what vistas lie ahead."

ANCIL LEA III

A Handwritten Letter

BY MARC WINCHESTER

When I was fifteen my father pulled me aside and said, "Son, you need to go to college, but your mother and I can only pay for the first year." Having worked since I was thirteen, I figured I could manage working and going to school at the same time.

Three years later things were a bit tougher. Determined not to go back to my father and ask for money I decided to get a third job to complement the two I was already working. I was already rising at 5:30 a.m. daily to clear and bus tables at UNC's Carolina Inn. The breakfast shift ended at 8:30, giving me time to head to campus for daily classes from 9:00 a.m. until noon. After classes I would grab a quick bite and run to the First Union National Bank where I worked daily from 1:00 to 5:00 p.m. as a courier.

To make ends meet I found one more role which was washing dishes (a recurring theme in my youthful employment) at The Pines, a high-end steak house, from 6:00 p.m. to 10:00-11:00 p.m. daily. I won't tell the gentle reader what I did from 11:00 p.m. to 5:30 a.m. every evening, just suffice it to say the small amount of studying I did allowed me to graduate only a semester late.

I wrote my best friend a long letter describing my plight and semi-despair. Then I went about my business.

About three weeks later I went to my Post Office box, and to my delight there was a personal handwritten note with a return address, a stamp, very nice stationary, everything. It was better than Christmas!

I can't begin to tell you how long it had been since I had seen a note addressed to me in the US Mail. Today, the average person receives one piece of personal mail about every eleven weeks. The personal touch has been replaced with rapidly disappearing text and email messages. Most likely had that been the medium of this communication I would not have it and likely would not remember it. The letter was too great to open and read right there, so I waited until I got off work at 11 o'clock.

Inside was a note from my best friend's father, a very successful real estate developer in Jacksonville, Florida, and a man who I had a tremendous amount of respect for. There was no check included in the envelope. However, there was something included which turned out to be worth much more than any check Mr. Skinner could have written me. And that was some great advice. Mr. Skinner wrote "Marc, in life, in business, in school, in marriage, and in sports there's always going to be good times and bad times. Smooth times and rough times."

"Anyone can get through the smooth times, but it takes a man or a woman of grit to get through the tough times. And if I could say one thing to you as you go through working these incredible hours and trying to get educated at the same time it would be this: Keep grinding. Keep going. Don't stop. Show some grit. Get through it. And when you do, you will look back from the other side and see there will be nothing in your future you will not be able to conquer."

Those were words a struggling young man of twenty needed to hear. An unexpected personal touch affirming my struggle was worthwhile, noble, and doable. And that I could get through it.

I did, and so did Mr. Skinner's note. It's framed and sits in the center of the mantel in my office. More importantly it remains in my heart. A piece of genuine care that I often share with others who are traveling a difficult path.

A note from Ancil:

Today, I still have a handwritten note from Marc inside my nightstand at home from when I was a sales rep years ago for a medical software company in which he was the CEO. He has always encouraged me and others in these sales roles to write these notes to our clients and prospects - they make a difference!

Start Small:
Grow Your Influence by Serving Others

Growing Your Circle of Influence

Whether you're at the beginning of your career, in the middle, or anywhere along the path, you must grow your circle of influence to have an impact for your product and get more business. The conventional wisdom on how to grow these connections is to join some networking organization. However, what I've really seen successful in growing my own circle of influence in life has been serving others. Whether in small ways or large, serving others grows your influence to a level that you often couldn't have comprehended.

You see, in order to be first, you really need to become last and put others first. In doing so, when you go out and serve others—whether it be volunteering for an event, to serve on a committee, to coach a soccer team, anything—it increases your level of contacts more than you can believe. Even serving others by making a difference in the life of a child through sponsorship in a children's home, becoming extended family for them, or perhaps considering foster care—the impact you have on people's lives somehow connects you to so, so many others who are down there in the trenches, digging and trying to help. And as you work shoulder to shoulder with them, you build a lasting bond.

By building these bonded relationships, you increase your number of connections, contacts, and friends several fold in ways you never could through some shallow networking organization. Beyond these growing connections, the blessings you receive by serving others first are tremendous in and of themselves. I personally consider that all the contacts are really just a side benefit to serving others. For me, the joy of helping someone is what gets me excited and blesses my heart. And, again, I've seen it proven true time and time again—when you bless others first and help meet their needs, you will in turn be blessed.

It's somewhat counterintuitive, but it is real and it is something you can easily do if you just take the first step and start small. You don't have to look for anything ginormous to begin. Simply find a place where you can begin to serve and start. The following few chapters are stories of how I've walked this out in my own life. I hope you'll see that a simple step forward is often all it takes.

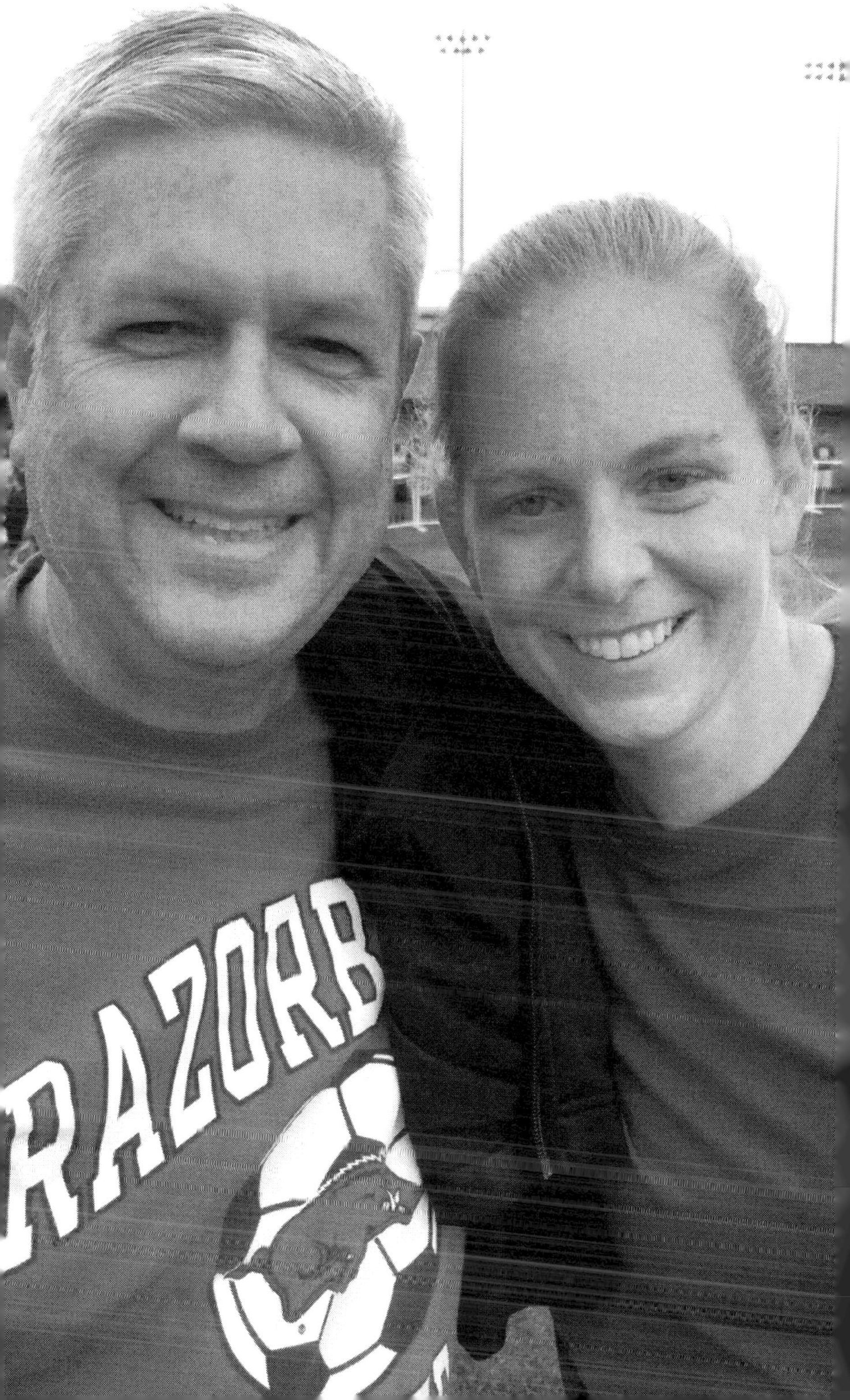
RAZORB

Mentoring

While I have worked in medical software technology for the last thirty-four years, I also have had other priorities in my life. One of these has been coaching. I have coached soccer both on a club and at a high school level for the last twenty-plus years and have enjoyed it thoroughly. Surprisingly, something that's mattered most to me for my success on and off the field has been the recruitment, development, and mentorship of my assistant coaches.

My second year of coaching high school girls soccer, I realized I needed a female assistant. Right away I contacted the athletic director of coaching for one of our local colleges and asked for a recommendation. He was in Rogers, Arkansas at a soccer clinic, and he introduced me to my first assistant coach, Abby.

Abby was a sophomore collegiate soccer player for a small college here in our town called Central Baptist College; she'd already had some experience coaching clinics in the summer. We visited with one another and quickly decided she would become my assistant.

As we approached our first season, I really laid out for her what I wanted her to do, including the training she needed. It was important for her to invest her time and energy into several licenses to be able to instruct well. She was a great collegiate soccer player, but she needed to be able to teach our players, put together a practice plan, and really help lead practice. So, she began the licensing process. Eventually, through our years coaching together, she got her D License, which qualifies her to coach competitively for all ages fourteen and up.

Over the course of five years, Abby greatly helped me and really became my right arm. She got to the point where she could really run things herself. It was kind of a glorious thing to see. I may have even convinced her to get her master's degree so she could stay around a while longer. She did! She got her master's degree in teaching while continuing to coach for us. Once she graduated, she actually came on full-time at the high school we coached for! She stayed there a year before being hired to be the assistant head coach of a much larger school in Northwest Arkansas.

One of the coolest things I remember closer to the end of our coaching together is when it seemed like we had the same mind. Both looking at the field, she would be standing ten steps in front of me on the touch line, and I'd be standing close to the bench. She couldn't see me. She couldn't read my facial expressions or know my thoughts. And suddenly something would happen on the field that needed to change. Without even turning around to look at me, she would say, "I hear you, coach." I hadn't said a word. But she saw what I saw and knew what needed to take place whether it was a substitution or we needed to move someone over. We both saw and knew together what adjustment was needed to be competitive and win.

We had several moments like that towards the end of our time together where we simply had the same mind. It was incredible.

About a year ago they did an article on her up in Northwest Arkansas. She'd won eight or nine state championships, both through coaching cross country and soccer. In the article, she made a very sweet, kind reference to me, which meant more than I can express.

Building into someone else is critical to success. Many call it mentorship. Some call it coaching. I'm not really sure what the best term is. But when you pour yourself and your knowledge into one of your team members, you will be successful. And more than successful—I can't tell you the amount of joy, of satisfaction, of fulfillment that you get from seeing others around you succeed and thrive. What a blessing.

I texted Abby this week to check on her, as I usually do. Though we haven't coached together in years, I still go up to her area to keep in touch and see how she's doing. She does the same, always reaching out whenever her team is playing down in my area. I'll meet her wherever the game is to watch her team play, enjoy seeing her coach, and give her a hug as we catch up. When I texted her this week, I just said, "Hey, how's my favorite coach?" She texted me back immediately, "Funny you should ask. I've got some big news," she wrote, alongside a picture of her engagement ring.

I can't tell you how proud I am of her and her success both on and off the field. Investing in others is a joy I highly recommend. It's not a bad thing to find ways to help yourself, but succeeding in this life means building into other's lives as well. I believe that if you help other people, you will be blessed and in a sense will be helping yourself.

Toad Suck Daze

I ran for mayor in our little town back in the late '90s. I did not win, but there were many good things that came out of that race that affected my life, and I feel like my team had a positive impact on the community through it all.

About a month after the race, I got a phone call from a very good friend of mine who I had grown up with. He put before me, "Hey Ancil, our committee has gotten together, and we would like to formally ask you and Lesley to become the co-chairs of Toad Suck Daze." I thanked him, and I told him we'd think about it. It was an honor to be considered, but I needed to talk to my wife, Lesley, and see if it was something we wanted to do. I would call him back.

So, after hanging up with him, I called my wife. "Hey," I said, "we've been asked to be co-chairs of Toad Suck Daze."

She replied immediately, "Absolutely, 100% yes!"

"Really?" I quizzed. "For sure," she said.

This position is a great honor in our city of about 75,000-100,000 people, as Toad Suck Daze is a unique-to-us festival that happens every year. To give you some background if you're not familiar with it, Toad Suck Daze is named now after a part of the Arkansas River that runs nearby. While a bridge connects our county to a neighboring one these days, in the past there was a ferry that would take people across the river, which is pretty swift, by the way.

Toad Suck was called that initially because back in the 1800s they would have barges coming up and down the river, and there were saloons on the far side of the river. Guys on the barges would pull over to get a drink, and it's said that they'd suck on the end of the bottle until they swelled up like toads. Thus, they called it Toad Suck.

Today, Toad Suck Daze is a local festival held the first week in May of every year. The proceeds from it go toward scholarship funds for seniors attending local colleges or universities. While it started out small, it's grown into something very large for our city, county, and even for the state. The focus of this is a family-friendly environment—lots of crafts, rides, entertainment, and a lot of music. It tracks probably anywhere from 200 to 300 thousand or more people to the event each year. We were even featured on late night with Jay Leno at least once. It's a giant festival, and it's always quite the undertaking.

Every year, they ask a couple to be the co-chairs and host the event. I realized quickly that being a co-chair meant a lot—both in responsibility and in honor. And so, I called my friend back and accepted the offer to be the next co-chairs of Toad Suck Daze.

In order to do so, we had to spend one year as an apprentice. The following year we would be the official co-chairs, and the third year we would be mentors to whoever took up the torch after us. So, probably only a month after I received this phone call, they asked us to start attending committee meetings. I admit, I didn't know what I was getting into when I accepted this role. The whole festival is designed and run by a large group of volunteers, somewhere between one and two hundred people. It was quite the model for volunteerism, as I spent lots of time both in committee meetings and in actually running the event itself. It took a great deal of organization, and

I learned much about volunteering and volunteerism.

One of the cool things that happened during this is that we got to know so, so many people. It was just incredible. I would easily guess many hundreds, if not thousands of people crossed paths with us by the end of Toad Suck Daze.

These relationships were one of the greatest benefits that came out of serving. We really had a blast, even with all the work involved. Getting to be backstage in concerts, being the PR representatives who were interviewed on TV and the radio—the whole thing was a lot of fun. But we also got to meet all these new friends!

And that's one of the things that I look back on and think about whenever people stop me around town and ask, "How do you know everybody in town?"

Years of service, really. Those years of serving through Toad Suck Daze—and countless other years of serving people—that is what has allowed me to know all these people. It's about serving first.

Toad Suck Daze was a blast and one of the best things I've ever done. My kids miss it to this day.

My Story — Helping Children in Need

My last semester of college, I happened to be walking through the student union when I was approached with a request. At the time I was a single dad just looking forward to finishing up my degree and getting off into my career. But as I was walking through the student union, someone stopped me and said, "Hey, we need a driver for the bus to take us over to the children's home," which was about two and a half hours away, over the river and through the woods. It caught me by surprise, this request to drive a 15-passenger van loaded with college students over to a children's home in order to do vespers for them and just interact with the kids.

And I know the reason they asked me was because I was a little bit older (I had gone and laid out during my college career for a year or two) I sure didn't have any great experience or license or anything, but this guy just felt compelled to ask me. I wasn't doing anything during the time they needed a driver and was actually feeling quite lonesome, so I thought, hey, this might be a good thing to do. I said yes.

So, I drove the group from college over to the children's home. We arrived, sang some songs for them and had a meal all together. The big moment for me came after we did all that and were getting ready to load up to return back to school. They simply asked us to go into the cottages and play with the kids. No big deal, right?

I entered one cottage, and it blew me away. I just hadn't anticipated this moment of sitting down on the floor, playing with these kids. I recall my cottage had younger children, maybe five and six year olds. All had come from homes or situations of abuse or neglect and were there through no fault of their own. Yet the kids kept telling me they wanted to go home. They talked about their parents. I was blown away that they missed home; they missed their parents. In my mind I wondered, would they ever get to go home? How would that look? I found myself pondering all these questions about their future.

After a while we left, getting back on the bus. But I was never the same. I'd seen the need of these kids who were there from all kinds of unbelievable circumstances. They'd been put in a home, almost like an orphanage, that cared for them, loved on them, nurtured them. This was a whole new experience for me to see up close and personal.

Back on campus, I finished up that last semester and got a great job selling medical software. I felt very blessed financially. But I never forgot that night at the children's home.

I decided to see if I could re-engage with them somehow. Making a few phone calls, I found out I could sponsor a child. It was simple—just giving money every month for their needs. So, I did that. I started sponsoring children even before I got remarried, which happened not too long after graduation.

The home would assign me a child, tell me about them and their needs, and I would give to that child. Soon, I started taking Christmas and birthday presents to them. My wife and I then started taking trips to the children's home in order to have a meal with our assigned child or simply take them somewhere. We would take them to McDonald's for a Happy Meal or go shopping at Walmart with them—any little fun things we could do in the span of a few hours. That was our start.

As time went by, we continued to get more involved as they would assign us new kids. Many times, the kids assigned to us would either leave that home or be reunited eventually with a family member who could care for them. We would be assigned a new child, and we simply continued taking them to dinner or out for their birthday. A few of the kids even wrote us letters, which was really cool.

Eventually, because of my involvement, they asked me to come on the board, which was over a whole network of children's homes in our state. I was honored to serve on that for several years while we continued to sponsor children. While I rotated off that board eventually, my wife and I continued our involvement with these homes. We would get our small group involved, doing simple things like pillow drives. I remember my wife driving down to one children's home with our whole family van stuffed full of brand-new pillows!

Years later, I was asked to join the board of another children's home, Soaring Wings. I knew they were doing great work, so once again, I said yes. I was on the board for at least two or three years before we had another significant step happen. One evening we were having dinner in one of the cottages after a board meeting. This was usual after a meeting in order for all the members to see and engage with the cottage, the home parents, and the kids.

After we got through eating, other members started talking about this concept called extended family. The program was such that you could host a child in your home one weekend a month and often a week at Christmas and a week during the summer. It wasn't any big deal; it was just providing a place where the kids could hang out. My wife and I left that dinner, got in the car, and I almost instantly said to my wife, "I think this sounds really interesting. What do you think?"

After discussion and prayerful consideration, we decided to give it a go. Most of our kids had graduated and gone off to school. We had empty bedrooms; we had space so that a child could have her own room and everything. We made the appropriate contacts, filled out all the applications, and were approved for the extended family program.

So we were assigned this little 9 year old girl, who needed a place to go 'hang out', watch TV, play with our dogs and eat pizza.

Who knew at that time, we'd end up adopting our little girl. It all started small.

I'm still thankful I was asked to drive that 15-passenger van all those years ago. And I'm thankful now and always to have 'our sweet girl' as a part of our family forever.

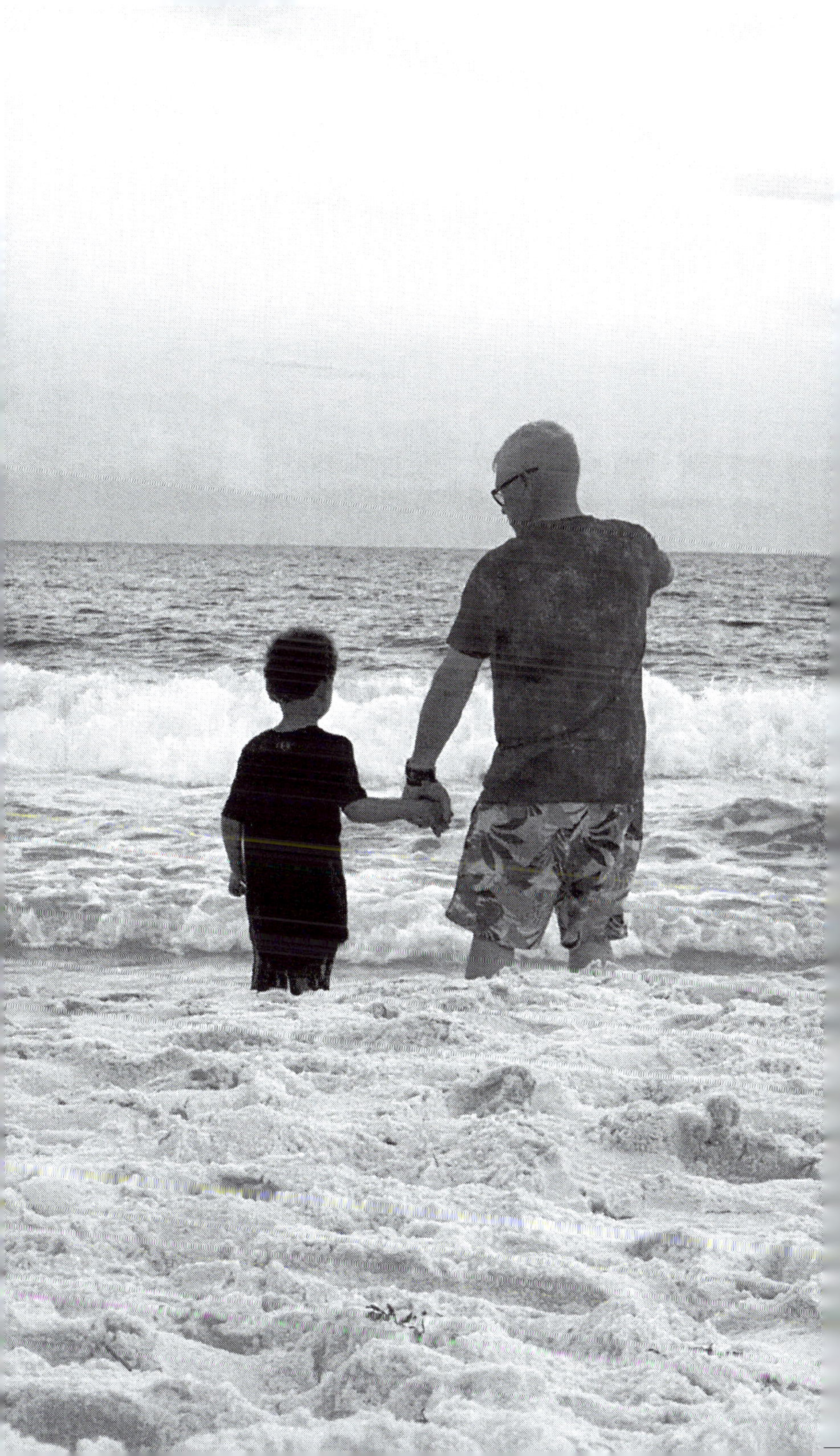

Wrapping Up

I was having coffee one morning with a friend of mine while we were on a project together. This 75-year-old, experienced technology guy looked at me and said, "Ancil, you like to help people. You need to help yourself."

Initially I thought, you know, he may be right. But then I decided to turn that around a little bit.

You see, I firmly believe that if I help people, I will help myself. That's been my mantra all along as I've gone through my career—that helping others comes back around to me somehow. Now, that's not why I've decided to prioritize helping others. I do it out of love for others. Love. It's an interesting word, simple but massive in meaning. I think that's what we are missing right now.

You can make all kinds of money. You can run over all kinds of people. But success without love is a very hollow thing. Sure, I have been run over during my career and taken advantage of a time or two, but I keep moving forward. From a starting place of love, I really want to see the other person succeed. Because if they succeed, I'll succeed, too.

I hope that you can glean something from this book that would help make you successful. Nothing would make me more happy than to get a message from you stating how this book has helped you succeed and become a better person. I hope sincerely, in the course of your work and career and life, that you can change the life of someone else for the better. You'll be blessed immensely, and that would be an awesome thing.

Please feel free to reach out to me if I can walk you through what that looks like or give you ideas on how to start small by investing in the lives of others whether it's through your community, in volunteerism, or in the life of a child. I'm happy to do that.

In the meantime, I pray your path is blessed and your troubles are few.

You Can Make A Difference

Thanks for investing the time to read this book. I hope you found it helpful to your life and work! Now go out there and implement! But before you do, please take a moment to leave a review on Amazon using the link below. It tells Amazon that people enjoy this book and lets other readers know they will benefit from it. **When you leave a review, you significantly better the chances for these stories to positively affect the hearts and minds of those who need them the most.** Any length or message will suffice. It would mean a lot. Thank you!

- Ancil

www.amazon.com/dp/B0B6GKG42N

CONTACT ME:
info@ancillea.com
LinkedIn: www.linkedin.com/in/ancillea/
Virtual cup of coffee - calendly.com/ancil
Happy to help you or your organization or team sell more! Coaching. Zoom webinars. Connections. Coffee.

Aperitif

Online training resources:
ancillea.com

Also available on Amazon:
Common Grounds: The Entrepreneur's Guide to the Coffee Shop Office

Coming soon:
Common Grounds 3: Selling into Healthcare

Made in the USA
Columbia, SC
02 August 2023